X32A
43.00 EC
16.25 US

W9-AED-134

Fishes of the Caribbean Reefs

Ian F. Took

CARIBBEAN

Macmillan Education
Between Towns Road, Oxford OX4 3PP
A division of Macmillan Publishers Limited
Companies and representatives throughout the world

www.macmillan-caribbean.com

ISBN 0 333 26969 1

Text © I. Took 1978

First published 1979

All rights reserved; no part of this publication may be
reproduced, stored in a retrieval system, transmitted in any
form or by any means, electronic, mechanical, photocopying,
recording, or otherwise, without the prior written permission
of the publishers.

Cover photograph courtesy of C. Huxley

Printed in Thailand

2005
25   24   23

Acknowledgements

I would like to thank the many diving friends who joined me on our
numerous underwater photographic forays, they assisted with location
of species and helped with identification.

Also, especial thanks must go to my wife, apart from typing the
manuscript, she patiently endured countless weekends as a 'diving
widow' while material was gathered for this book.

All photographs were taken by the author.

Contents

Introduction   1

Practical Fishwatching   4

The Coral Reef   9

Conservation   16

The Fishes   19
Descriptive text and illustrations covering 85 species

Underwater Photography   84

Index   91

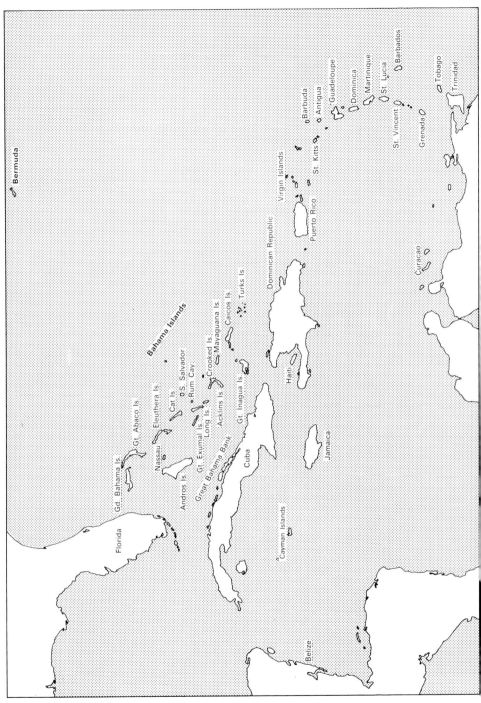

A map of the Caribbean

Introduction

The main purpose of this book is to provide the keen diver and snorkeller with an introduction to some of the more common and spectacular fish which can be seen around the Caribbean and Tropical West Atlantic Reefs. It should also be of interest to those who maintain marine aquaria, as many of the smaller species covered are quite suitable for the average home aquarium.

I have attempted to include representatives of most of the major families, but due to the difficulties encountered in photographing some otherwise common species underwater, and the element of time, this small guide is of necessity limited in coverage. It is to be hoped that a more comprehensive guide can be produced at a later date.

Text has been kept to a minimum, and is confined to a brief description of the fishes in question, where they are likely to be found, general habits, and any characteristics particularly of size, shape and colouration that will lead to easier identification.

Most of the material for this book has been gathered from the East Caribbean area, but the majority of the species covered are widespread and occur as far as Bermuda in the north and the Atlantic coast of Brazil in the south, as well as within the whole of the Caribbean area.

Unless otherwise stated, all of the photographic illustrations were taken underwater. They show the fish in their normal environment and in natural colour.

Colouration of fish can however sometimes cause problems with identification. Many species exhibit varying colour phases, while others can change colour or pattern more or less instantaneously, either to suit the background shade or through fear.

In addition there is often great variation in both colour and shape between juvenile and adult fish, and between the male and female of the same species.

Where these variations can be extreme, more than one photograph is shown, or notes are made in the text. The shallow water snorkeller may indeed only see the juveniles of some species as the adult fish frequently move off into deeper waters. In these cases, the illustrations may show the juvenile stage only. Overall shape is usually the most distinctive feature, followed by colouration and markings.

Different species have their own favourite habitats; and while some are widespread, others are more or less strictly confined to specific areas, ie. sandy bottoms, caves etc. As with other forms of wildlife, this specific distribution is largely governed by feeding habits, and prior knowledge of this factor will give you a good idea of the species to be found in any particular locality.

While we talk broadly about 'Reef fish' this does not always mean fish which live on or around actual living coral reefs.

Many types of sea bed occur, from large expanses of apparently featureless sand and shingle, coral rubble, and old eroded reef tops, to areas of 'sea grass', rocky gullies and boulders (particularly around islands of volcanic origin). The actual living coral reef itself may only form a small part of the whole.

In addition, various manmade underwater habitats: old wrecks, sea walls, jetties and piles, often provide the very best hunting ground for the keen fishwatcher. As mentioned earlier, many species can be found in all the above locations while others are more specific. As an example, if you want to find and study the Goatfishes (Mullidae), look for areas of sand, mud and shingle. These fish are bottom feeders and will rarely be found over reefs or over hard rocky areas, unless they are well interspersed with sand-filled gullies.

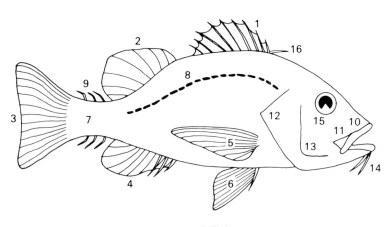

1 First dorsal fin	9 Finlets
2 Second dorsal fin	10 Pre-maxilla
3 Caudal fin	11 Maxilla
4 Anal fin	12 Operculum
5 Pectoral fin	13 Pre-opercle
6 Pelvic fin	14 Barbels
7 Caudal peduncle	15 Cheek
8 Lateral line	16 Horizontal spine before first dorsal fin

The parts of a bony fish

Another example is the Copper or Glassy Sweeper, *Pempheris schomburgki*. This attractive little schooling fish is usually found in caves, under deep coral ledges, or inside wrecks. It rarely ventures far during the daytime.

In describing an individual fish in this book the common name or names are given, together with the scientific name. Sizes shown do not denote minimum or maximum sizes, but merely indicate the average overall lengths of the fish likely to be seen in shallow coastal waters.

The chapter following deals with practical aspects of fishwatching in more detail and is aimed mainly at the newcomer to snorkelling, there are also short chapters on the coral reef and on conservation. There is a chapter on aspects of underwater photography at the end of the book. It is to be hoped that once you have learned to see, you will want to capture a permanent record.

Fish can be likened to birds, in that observation of both has much in common, the only difference being the environment in which they live. If you can adapt yourself in some small measure to the fish's environment, it can open up a whole new world and provide enough material for a lifetime of study and enjoyment.

Practical Fishwatching

If you are new to fishwatching and have no experience of snorkelling, a few hints on the equipment needed and the practical aspects involved are necessary.

Basic equipment

The only absolutely essential pieces of equipment for fishwatching are a suitable face mask and a snorkel tube, although to make life easier we should also include a pair of fins.

The really important thing is that all equipment should fit comfortably. You may be spending hours at a time in the water, so take some time in choosing your equipment carefully.

There is a vast range of face masks available, but the important features are comfort in use, the ability to form a watertight seal on the face, and that it is fitted with tempered or laminated glass.

The snorkel tube must fit comfortably in your mouth without chafing and should be of the simple open-ended type. Do not be tempted by models with ball valves or any other fancy features.

Fins should be comfortable and not too tight a fit. Models with a built-in heel are preferable to those with adjustable heel straps, since you will often be walking over rough and sharp rocks, not to mention the odd, and well concealed sea urchin!

Other 'basic equipment' for tropical areas must include an old 'T' shirt or something similar, and possibly an old soft hat of some kind. These last are essential for protection against sunburn unless you are already well acclimatised. The shoulders and the back of the neck are particularly susceptible, and there is no point in ruining an expensive holiday for the sake of a few simple precautions.

A glove or pair of gloves are recommended if you are going to handle rocks or coral. Some can inflict deep cuts on unprotected hands and others can 'sting' quite painfully. A household rubber glove will do, or for heavier duty one of the many types of gardening gloves will offer excellent protection.

If you are completely new to snorkelling, spend an hour or two in a swimming pool or some other shallow calm area, getting used to your new equipment. It may feel strange at first, but with practice you will pick up the technique very quickly.

Practical aspects of snorkelling

Before snorkelling, or indeed swimming in any area which is unknown to you, do check with local people or the local authorities about such things as currents and tides. This particularly applies to aqualung divers who may well be in deeper waters, perhaps a mile or two offshore.

It is also essential that you are aware of any local conservation laws which may prohibit the taking of coral or shells etc., or which may require a permit before you can snorkel or dive.

Be particularly careful about walking or swimming out through heavy surf. Unless you are a strong and experienced snorkeller it is better to avoid these areas altogether and look for calmer waters. Having gone out through surf over the reef, remember that you will have to come back, and this can be even more hazardous.

Finally be very wary in areas where other water sports are practised. This mainly applies to power boats and water skiers, but in general it is wise to keep away from all areas where sailing dinghies and other craft are in evidence.

Some potential hazards

Generally speaking, snorkelling is a relaxing and completely safe pastime, and one which can be enjoyed by young and old alike. In all tropical waters however there are some possible dangers, and it is well to be aware of these.

Sunburn
This has already been mentioned, the danger is a very real one until you have developed a good suntan. Suntan oils or lotions offer no protection while snorkelling as they are washed off almost at once.

Surface craft
Keep your eyes and ears open, remember that you will not be very visible to a boat driver, and the safest course is to keep well away from all areas occupied by surface craft, and in particular ski boats.

Dangers underfoot
In certain areas you will have to walk out some way before reaching water of swimming depth. Fortunately the Caribbean does not enjoy the presence of highly venomous creatures such as the Stonefish, but minor hazards do exist and under no circumstances should you walk over coral rubble, or reef areas in bare feet.

5

Sea urchins abound in places, and corals can be sharp and in some cases sting badly. Fins with a built-in heel offer good protection, and by shuffling out slowly, preferably backwards, until you reach water deep enough to swim, you should have no problems.

Some specific hazards

Sea urchins

These are in evidence almost everywhere. The long spined varieties are particularly dense in places and all care should be taken to avoid standing on them or touching them. The spines are not normally poisonous but are extremely sharp and brittle, and once embedded in the skin will break off and are almost impossible to remove. Usually no infection results but they can cause considerable pain if embedded in the heel, and it may well be several weeks before they are completely absorbed by the body.

Coral cuts and grazes

These are by far the most common minor injuries and a permanent feature of the underwater photographer's life.

Many live corals are extremely sharp, and cuts may not be immediately obvious while in the water. Infection can start very easily, and as cuts and grazes can take some time to heal, it is essential that a mild antiseptic be applied as soon as possible after washing the wound.

Stinging corals

Certain species of Fire Coral, *Millepora* spp. are common in the Caribbean, and are usually found on old shallow eroded reef tops (see Figures 5 and 6). They are also found as encrustations on old wrecks and other manmade objects. Fire Corals occur in several forms but can usually be recognised by their smooth yellow to yellowish brown appearance, with edges commonly tipped in white. The sting may be painful and can itch for several days. Although not poisonous as such, an antiseptic should be applied and a watch kept for any local infection. As with insect bites, avoid scratching if possible.

Jellyfish and allied species

At certain times of the year, the water may carry a heavy concentration of almost invisible **stinging plankton**. The first awareness you will have is a sensation of tiny pin pricks. These are more annoying than dangerous, although at times there may be so many that it will be unpleasant to stay in the water. No one likes swimming through a bed of nettles.

Of the jellyfish, and allied species, only the ubiquitous Portuguese Man O' War need be taken seriously in the Caribbean. It is easily recognised by its bright blue 'float', and has long tentacles well-endowed with stinging cells.

If you are unfortunate enough to be stung by the Man O' War, which can be like a red hot whip lash, leave the water immediately and bathe the affected area with *alcohol*. Methylated spirits, or at a pinch, gin and vodka, are satisfactory substitutes. Do *not* attempt to wash the stings off with fresh water as this will cause any remaining stinging cells to discharge into the skin. Medical attention may be necessary if the patient is shocked.

Other Caribbean jellyfish can sting but the effect is minor when compared with the Man O' War. Small specimens are sometimes referred to as 'Blue Bottles' and although perhaps only an inch or so across the float, can still deliver a painful sting.

Shells
Some species of cone shell possess a highly venomous barb which has on occasion proved lethal. Unless you are able to make a positive identification and know how to pick them up, leave all cone shells well alone.

Fish with venomous or sharp spines
Fortunately there are no lethal species in the Caribbean, but a few sting badly, and nasty cuts can result if certain fish are handled carelessly.

Scorpionfish (*Scorpoenidae*) There are several species in the area, all of which are extremely well-camouflaged, and at first glance, very similar in appearance. They are common in certain localities, particularly on old eroded reef tops, in coral rubble, and around wrecks, jetties and other manmade obstructions. The main danger lies in the fact that they are so well-camouflaged and generally motionless. It is quite easy to stand on one or put a hand on one without seeing it. Most possess venomous spines along the dorsal and head area and stings are liable to be deep and painful. Immediate first aid consists of immersing the affected area in water as hot as the patient can bear, and this treatment should be continued until the pain subsides. Medical aid should be sought as soon as possible.

Several other fish, while not venomous, do have sharp bony spines or plates which can inflict cuts if carelessly handled. Among these are the Surgeon fishes (Acanthuridae) which have sharp 'scalpels' immediately behind the caudal fin, Angelfish and Squirrelfish with their sharp pre-opercula spines, and several species equipped with bony dorsal spines which are capable of inflicting pricks and cuts.

Handle all unknown species carefully even if dead.

All Stingrays should be approached with utmost caution, especially large specimens. They are equipped with one or two venomous serrated spines at the base of the tail, and if approached from a head-on position can bring the tail over the body and lash the intruder. The venomous sting is large, and cuts can be deep and extremely painful. Since infection is quite likely, medical aid should be sought promptly.

Fish that bite

Many fish can bite, and even the pretty little Damselfishes will 'attack' the snorkeller with gusto if he intrudes into their territory.

Uppermost in most minds however, will be the shark, which is certainly the most potentially dangerous of all sea creatures. It is not intended to dwell on, or discuss, the shark in this book. You are unlikely to see one in shallow coastal reef areas, and even if you do, it is unlikely to cause you any trouble. Having said that, if you do see one, leave the water as quickly and as quietly as possible. The shark and its habits are still little understood and discretion is always the better part of valour.

Barracuda This fearsome-looking fish seems to have a reputation that is probably not justified. It is certainly well-equipped to bite severely but no real evidence exists that can place it as a serious hazard.

When aqualung diving, it is not uncommon to find oneself among a large shoal of small barracuda or to come face to face with a large solitary specimen. They may hang around with mouths agape and even approach and circle, but any recorded actual 'attacks' are probably the result of their being attracted to fish on a spearfisherman's belt, or some other small shiny object.

Moray eels Eels are abundant in most locations, but particularly on eroded reefs, old wrecks, piles and jetties etc. Again they seem to have an undeserved reputation and in the writer's experience are not aggressive unless unduly provoked. The moral is, as with all sea creatures, do not annoy them and they are unlikely to bother you. Morays have sharp teeth and can bite severely if the mood so takes them.

Many other fish are capable of biting, even small and harmless-looking species, but the chances of this occurring are extremely remote unless you are handling freshly caught specimens.

Mention must be made of the friendly octopus, again the subject of undeserved folklore. A really large specimen is capable of biting and possibly holding down someone foolish enough to place a hand or arm in its lair. They are however highly intelligent creatures and can generally be handled quite safely – if you can catch one! A game of hide and seek with a fleeing octopus is an experience all should enjoy. They are masters of camouflage and subterfuge and you will need to be very keen-eyed to keep up the game for long.

Having discussed some of the potential hazards, it is fair to say that the worst thing likely to happen is the odd coral cut, or chance contact with a sea urchin.

Apart from some species of shark, sea creatures are not aggressive if not provoked or threatened. Keep your eyes open, do not put your hands into holes or cracks, and as a general rule, watch rather than touch.

The Coral Reef

Many and various phrases have been used to describe the beauty of coral reefs, but perhaps 'coral garden' best describes the scene for those of us who are familiar with it.

Broadly confined between the latitudes of the Tropic of Cancer and the Tropic of Capricorn, and forming mainly on the eastern shores of continental land masses, coral reefs typically fall into one of three recognised forms.

The *Fringing Reef*, which is usually an extension of the land mass, and has shallow lagoonal waters only, between land and reef. One of the finest examples is the fringing system along the East Coast of Africa.

The *Barrier Reef* is generally several miles offshore, and separated from the land mass by deep water channels. Here the Great Australian Barrier Reef is perhaps the finest example.

The distinction between these two classes often seems hazy, and it appears that both types can occur together, or overlap somewhat as in some areas of the Caribbean.

Lastly is the *Atoll*, which is essentially a ring-shaped reef system enclosing a lagoon. This form has resulted from either the subsidence of an island within an earlier barrier reef system, a fall in sea level or a combination of both.

The coral reef itself is made up almost entirely of living and dead animals, the live corals and allied species forming a living cap over the dead foundation of the reef structure itself. This has been laid down over countless centuries, mainly from the limestone skeletons of stony corals, but also from the remains of many other related animal species that grow on and form a part of every coral reef.

On a typical healthy reef you will find many varieties of the true 'stony corals', together with other allied hard corals, and many widely differing forms of gorgonians, soft corals and sponges.

All are members of the animal kingdom and except for the sponges are known as **Coelenterates**. Sea anemones, hydroids, and jellyfish are all part of this same group.

True 'stony corals' belong to the Class *Anthozoa* and it is the calcareous skeletons of these animals which make up the bulk of any reef structure.

The individual coral animal or *polyp* is a simple tubular-shaped creature with a large digestive tract and a fringe of stinging tentacles around the 'mouth'. These are used to entrap minute plankton which form the major part of its food. Each polyp lives in its own protective limestone cup which is formed from secreted lime, and examination of a piece of coral will reveal the hundreds of individual coral cups which make up a typical coral colony. Individual polyps reproduce either by 'budding off', as do some anemones, or by releasing fertilised eggs which develop into small larvae or *planulae*. These, if they survive, will eventually settle on some suitable rock or other hard substrate, and develop into individual polyps, each with its own limestone cup. Eventually through budding off, a new coral colony will be formed.

The polyps of true 'stony corals' all have six tentacles or multiples of six, and some of the more common and spectacular Caribbean species are listed below.

1 Staghorn Coral *Acropora cervicornus*

Often found in extensive beds down to around 40 feet (12 metres). In sheltered waters it may grow 6–8 feet (1.8–2.4 metres) in height. It is extremely delicate and suffers severely from wave action. Anchoring over beds of Staghorn can cause untold damage.

2 Elkhorn Coral *Acropora palmata*   Figure 1

Forms extensive beds, usually in very shallow waters, and may be awash at low tides. It forms broader branches and is more 'tree like' than *cervicornus*. Less susceptible to wave action, it may take on a variety of forms.

3 Finger Coral *Porites porites*   Figure 2

Several species, they grow only a few inches high and resemble a knobbly finger. Found in extensive beds in the 20–40 feet (6–12 metres) depth range.

Figure 1   Elkhorn Coral, *Acropora palmata*

Figure 2   Finger Coral, *Porites* sp.

4 Star Coral *Montastrea* spp.   Figure 28

Very common and taking many forms. Grows in boulder form often many
feet across. Extensive beds of interlocking Star Coral boulders are common
in 15–30 feet (4.5–9.0 metres) of water.

5 Brain Coral *Diploria labyrinthiformis*   Figure 3

As the name suggests these corals resemble the interior of a human brain.
There are many species, often difficult to identify, and they form in
boulders from a few inches to several feet across.

Figure 3   Brain Coral, *Diploria labyrinthiformis*

6 Pillar Coral *Dendrogyra cylindrus*   Figure 4

Not so widespread as Brain Coral, but often locally common. It is one of
the most spectacular species and in favoured areas can grow to 10 feet
(3 metres) or more in height. More usually 2–5 feet (0.6–1.5 metres) high.

Figure 4   Pillar Coral, *Dendrogyra cylindrus*

Figure 5   Fire Coral, *Millepora complanata*

7 Fire Coral *Millepora complanata*   Figure 5

Not a true stony coral, as it lacks the typical coral cups. Very common and widespread in shallow waters, where it grows in abundance on old eroded

Figure 6   Branching Fire Coral, *Millepora alcicornus*

reef tops, wrecks etc. *M. alcicornus* (Figure 6) is a branching species often found growing on dead sea fans and other gorgonians. Beware! Both can sting quite painfully.

Growing in and amongst all coral reefs and on adjacent sand and shingle flats you will find a great variety of what at first sight appear to be feathery plants.

These are in fact living animals, and are varieties of gorgonia and other soft corals.

Like the hard corals they are colonies of living polyps, but forming around a hard, horny tree-like structure. Unlike stony corals, each polyp captures food for the benefit of the entire colony.

The Common Sea Fan (Figure 7) is perhaps the most easily identified in shallow waters, and the sea-whips and precious 'black coral' of deeper waters are well known to aqualung divers.

Figure 7   Common Sea Fan, *Gorgonia ventalina*

Varieties of sponges, **Porifera**, almost complete the underwater land-scape. These will vary from brightly coloured encrusting growths on rocks and coral, to the often gigantic bath and vase sponges which can grow to heights of 5–6 feet (1.5–1.8 metres).

In amongst this beautiful and varied seascape lives a variety of marine animals that almost defies description.

This small guide deals only with fish, and the following pages will describe and illustrate some of the more common species you are likely to see.

Conservation

A popular and somewhat emotive word nowadays, conservation seems to imply a balancing act between the struggles of nature to survive on the one hand, and the ravages of man, for economic gain and progress on the other hand.

With the world's ever-growing industrial base, its expanding search for minerals and other natural resources, and an ever increasing number of mouths to feed, nature is accorded little respect, and is slowly but surely being eroded.

One has only to look at scarred landscapes and polluted rivers and lakes, to realise the damage that has, and still is, being created, for the sake of what we choose to call progress.

Is conservation a necessity or is it something we reluctantly think about after the damage has been done? In many cases governments will have to effect a careful balance between immediate economic gain, and possible long term irreversible effects on the environment. It is very often both an economic and political issue, and those who feel strongly enough about conservation in all its forms, must be prepared to put forward the strongest possible arguments for its enactment if it is to be practised on a wide enough scale.

We are concerned here with the sea, and more particularly with shallow coastal waters; their associated coral reefs, and the multitude of fish and other marine life which form part of this habitat. It is a finely balanced environment, and conditions for optimum growth and well being are easily upset. Evidence of this fact is unfortunately very obvious in many parts of the world where human population is high and industry is established.

Coral reefs can only form and thrive if certain conditions are met. They require light, optimum water temperatures of between 25–28 °C, clean, clear water free of unnatural impurities and excess suspended matter, and a high oxygen content.

Anything that interferes with this balance can cause a slowing down in growth or in extreme cases, rapid death of all coral polyps and departure of the reef inhabitants. The final result is a lifeless mound of rubble.

If we consider specific causes, the following forms of pollution, or interference with normal conditions, all have a harmful effect on living coral and reef structures.

Sewage effluent of all kinds, particularly if untreated, is very harmful. This includes human and domestic waste which in many countries is run straight into the sea, or into river systems feeding into the sea.

Industrial waste from factories and process plants is probably one of the worst offenders, so also to a lesser degree is run-off from agricultural chemicals and pesticides, particularly where these are applied in high concentration on land adjacent to the coast.

In some areas of the world *overgrazing* and *clearance of vegetation* has caused severe erosion around river systems, resulting in a heavy outpouring of silt and other suspended matter. Where coral reefs have formed around river mouths and in downstream coastal areas, the effect can be disastrous.

Large *oil spills* present a horrifying potential hazard, but continual minor leakages, and cleansing of tanks at sea, all contribute to a gradual build-up of pollutants. The widespread use of detergents to emulsify oil slicks probably has a worse effect on coastal marine life than the oil itself.

Large *coastal engineering schemes* can also have their harmful side effects, land reclamation, harbour works, diversion of water courses and creation of stagnant water areas by interruption of the normal flow of currents. All of these, unless carefully planned, can result in the demise of large areas of adjacent coral reef.

In addition to this indirect and perhaps not immediately obvious damage, there is the physical destruction of reefs by certain forms of trawl net fishing, dragging of boat anchors, and in some places widespread destruction of reef areas by coral collectors, for sale to tourists, and export to all corners of the world.

Apart from this manmade destruction, corals have their own natural enemies to contend with.

Fishes with long, pointed snouts and protruding beak-like teeth are fond of coral polyps, and some species of Butterflyfish and Filefish can be seen gently nibbling away to extract the soft polyps from their stony home.

Parrotfishes cause considerable damage to many varieties of corals. They will scrape deep gouges in Brain and Star Corals to extract the living matter, and bite off large pieces of branching coral. It has been calculated that much of the sand on coral beaches comes from the gut of Parrotfishes.

Pufferfish and Triggerfish have similar hard beak-like teeth and are also guilty of breaking off and chewing small pieces of coral.

Some starfish can and do feed on coral polyps, particularly rounded and plate-like forms. The Crown of Thorns starfish is probably the most notorious in this respect in Indo-Pacific regions, and it has caused considerable reef damage around the Australian East Coast in recent years.

Coral polyps are very intolerant of freshwater and coral formations around river mouths are very susceptible at times of heavy flooding.

In many instances the awareness of a need for conservation does not become apparent until it is almost too late. It should not, however, be regarded merely as a means of saving or protecting what is left, but should also be considered as a means of rejuvenating and improving what has already been damaged or polluted.

If the environment is made fit again much can be done to reverse the process of decay.

Coral growth is slow, but living corals will return even to dead reefs if the conditions for re-growth are suitable. A great deal can be done to improve barren areas by laying down artificial reefs. These will soon attract a large cross section of marine life, from fish and crustacea, to sponges, hydroids and soft corals. They will also form a base on which the stony corals can grow again. One has only to snorkel over a sunken wreck to see the vast array of marine life that it supports.

Experimental reefs have been created from all sorts of manmade materials. Concrete blocks, concrete pipes, old motor car and truck tyres and even complete car and truck bodies have been used. All have been successful to some extent and within a year or two they will attract a substantial fish population. Some materials will be colonised so rapidly by sponges and corals that they will be virtually unrecognisable after a few years.

Marine parks and reserves

Countries fortunate enough to have surrounding coral reefs must do all possible to ensure their protection and continuity. At the very least fully protected areas should be created, and designated as Marine Parks or Marine Reserves. These areas should be carefully delineated, and as with land based game and nature reserves, conditions of entry should be strictly laid down and enforced.

All of this costs money, but it will at least ensure continuity of a priceless natural asset and give endless pleasure to those fortunate enough to enjoy it.

In many countries creation of Marine Parks has led to increased tourism and hence increased revenue, and their value as areas for scientific research has proved invaluable.

Several Caribbean countries have adopted a policy of Marine Conservation. In Australia, U.S.A., Kenya, Seychelles and many other countries, Marine Parks have now been long established, and highly successful.

The sea is only slowly unfolding its secrets, let us not destroy this last great nature reserve, nor deny the pleasure it gives to present and future generations.

The Fishes

The following 85 species represent a cross section of most major families of fish and include some of the more common and attractive fishes likely to be seen over the average reef and in adjacent shallows.

Deep water, ocean-going fishes such as the Sharks, Jacks, and larger Snappers have not been covered; neither have the large families of Gobies and Blennies. By virtue of their small size and secretive habits, the latter are unlikely to be seen in numbers, or arouse much interest in the average observer. Likewise the larger ocean-going fishes will normally only be seen well offshore by aqualung divers or fishermen.

The keen student will find wider coverage and more detailed anatomical descriptions of West Atlantic and Caribbean fishes in the publications listed below.

1   Fishes of the Bahamas and Adjacent Tropical Waters
    James E. Bohlke and Charles C. G. Chaplin,
    Livingstone Publishing Company,
    Wynnewood, U.S.A.

2   Caribbean Reef Fishes,
    John E. Randall,
    T.F.H. Publications Inc.,
    Neptune City,
    New Jersey, U.S.A.

Spotted Moray   *Gymnothorax moringa*   Figure 8

Length 24–48″ (60–120cm)

By far the most common and widespread moray eel in the Caribbean shallows. In common with most morays it has long, needle-sharp canine teeth and large specimens present an awesome appearance on first contact. Colouration is usually whitish to pale yellow, with a densely mottled pattern of black to dark brown irregular spots and blotches. Can be found over all reef areas, under coral heads, large sponges and in coral rubble.

Normally seen with its head protruding from a hole or recess, often with mouth agape. In the writer's experience, morays are not aggressive if not provoked unduly and can quite safely be approached to within two or three feet. They are said to feed mainly on fish.

Goldentail Moray   *Muraena miliaris*   Figure 9

Length 12–20″ (30–50cm)

A small and relatively common moray eel found over most reefs and coral rubble areas. Colouration is dark brown, covered with densely-packed small yellow spots. The tail has larger yellow spots and blotches and may be entirely yellow at the tip. Typically seen with head protruding from holes and cracks in coral.

The largest moray in our area, the **Green Moray,** *Gymnothorax funebris,* is unlikely to be seen in very shallow waters. It prefers old wrecks and deeper clefts in reef drop-offs. Colouration is olive green/brown and this species can reach a length of at least 6 feet (1.8 metres) with a thick muscular body to match. Again despite its awesome size and appearance the writer has not experienced any real signs of aggression even when approaching this species quite closely.

Goldspotted Snake Eel   *Myrichthys oculatus*   Figure 10

Length 15–30″ (37–75cm)

The most attractive of the snake eels, this species is most likely to be noticed in the shallows. While all snake eels live in shallow burrows under the sand, *M. oculatus* will be frequently found gliding across sand flats, and in and around coral rubble, and sea grass beds. Body colour is various shades of yellow with very prominent bright yellow spots ringed in dark brown or black. Food consists of small crabs and other crustaceans.

Snake eels are frequently reported as sea snakes, but the West Indies has no known species. The Goldspotted Snake Eel is not aggressive and has been handled by the writer and his diving colleagues underwater without any adverse reaction. It seems in fact to have a gentle and inquisitive disposition.

Figure 8   Spotted Moray, *Gymnothorax moringa*

Figure 9   Goldentail Moray, *Muraena miliaris*

Figure 10   Goldspotted Snake Eel, *Myrichthys oculatus*

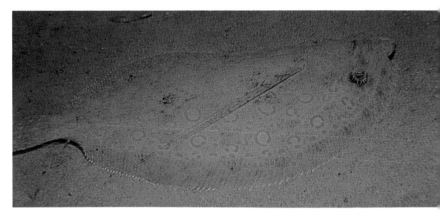

Figure 11   Peacock Flounder, *Bothus lunatus*

Figure 12   Trumpetfish, *Aulostomus maculatus*

Figure 13   Sand Diver, *Synodus intermedius*

Peacock Flounder *Bothus lunatus* Figure 11

Length 8–12″ (20–30cm)

Only one flounder is covered here. It is the most common in our area and is certainly the most colourful. It has both eyes on the left hand side of the head. It is common on soft, silty bottoms and among sea grass beds. Flounders are great colour changers and can alter colour to suit the background shade at will. Colouration varies from almost white to a dark brown/grey, and in darker colour phases the body is covered with bright blue dots, rings and open circles. The dorsal fin is long, and fully erected when the fish is moving rapidly. It will often bury itself in the sand, and has on frequent occasions been observed perched on top of coral boulders. Food consists of small fish, crustaceans etc. Not easy to see unless moving.

Trumpetfish *Aulostomus maculatus* Figure 12

Length 18–30″ (45–75cm)

A common and quite unmistakeable fish and the only species in the Caribbean. It is apparently abundant in all areas, around coral reefs and especially in dense stands of gorgonians. Shape is unmistakeable but this species is a great colour changer. The commonest colouration is reddish-brown with pale lateral lines and vague spots and bars. Other colour phases can be blue/grey, bright yellow (rarer), and various intermediate colours and shades. One large specimen observed developed several rows of brilliant green iridescent spots. It is carnivorous and will frequently be found hanging head down among large gorgonians to avoid detection. Relatively easy to approach but usually turns away from the observer.

Sand Diver *Synodus intermedius* Figure 13

Length 8–12″ (20–30cm)

The most common of the Lizardfishes in our area, it can be found in all areas on sand and shingle bottoms, and more rarely on live reefs. Large numbers are often found around old wrecks, jetties and large isolated coral heads where there are schools of small Grunts, Snappers and other fish on which it feeds.

Normally seen resting on the bottom (sometimes partially buried) on its ventral fins in a typical head-up pose, and while appearing lethargic, it can move with astonishing speed when after prey. It has a cavernous mouth with needle-sharp teeth, and will sometimes take a fish little smaller than itself. Large prey are turned endwise and the fish is slowly engorged in a snake-like fashion, usually tail first.

Its mottled brownish-green appearance, and the ability to change shade to match the bottom makes it difficult to see from above. Easily approached.

Squirrel fishes   *Holocentridae*

Also included in this family are the two Soldierfishes, *Myripristis jacobus* and *Plectrypops retrospinis*. All are very spiny reef fishes varying in colour from pale shades of pink to bright red. The Squirrelfishes are distinguished by sharp pre-opercular spines which are not found on the Soldierfishes. All have very sharp, spinous dorsal fins and should be handled with care even if dead.

Although generally nocturnal in habit, some species do roam around during daylight hours. Food consists mainly of small crustaceans. They can be found in small or large schools under rocky ledges, inside caves and wrecks, as well as in large congregations close to coral heads, often in close association with Grunts and small Snappers.

Squirrelfish   *Holocentrus rufus*   Figure 14

Length 6–12" (15–30cm)

One of the largest and most common of the Squirrelfishes, often seen singly or in small, well-dispersed groups. It seems less nocturnal than others of the family and will frequently be seen in the open although not far from cover. Colour ranges from a silvery-pink to light red, with indistinct light red blotches. The dorsal fin has sharp, well-defined spines with distinct white triangles along the top margins. These are absent on the Longjaw Squirrelfish which is otherwise very similar in appearance. The rear dorsal fin is long and well-developed and often appears filamentous in large specimens. Feeds mainly on small crustaceans and is considered to be good eating. It is not particularly wary and with care can be approached quite easily.

Longjaw Squirrelfish   *Holocentrus ascensionis*   Figure 15

Length 6–10" (15–25cm)

A very common Squirrelfish but one that is easily confused with *H. rufus*. Body shape and overall colouration is silvery-red with indistinct bars and blotches of a lighter or darker colour. The spiny dorsal fin does *not* bear the typical white-tipped margins which are a feature of *H. rufus*. Both species are often found together over reefs, coral heads, and wrecks. Occurs in small groups or singly and being nocturnal is always found close to cover during daylight hours. With care can be quite easily approached.

Figure 14　Squirrelfish, *Holocentrus rufus*

Figure 15　Longjaw Squirrelfish, *Holocentrus ascensionis*

Figure 16 Longspine Squirrelfish, *Flammeo marianus*

Figure 17 Blackbar Soldierfish, *Myripristis jacobus*

Dusky Squirrelfish *Holocentrus vexillarius*

Length 3–6" (7.5–15cm)

A common smaller species of the very shallow reefs. Colouration is more subdued than the other Squirrelfishes, with alternating silver and brownish-red horizontal stripes separated by fine, darker lines. There is a red spot at the root of the pectoral fins. Although common this species tends to stay in close proximity to coral and coral heads, often in the deeper clefts and recesses. It is very rarely observed swimming in the open during daylight hours.

Longspine Squirrelfish *Flammeo marianus* Figure 16

Length 4–6" (10–15cm)

A smaller and apparently rarer species, at least in shallow water, it is usually seen singly, or in small groups in and around coral heads and recesses in the reef. The overall impression of colour is distinctly orange, although the body colour is silver with closely-packed, horizontal, orange stripes running the length of the body. The dorsal fin is orange/red, again tipped with white triangles. A distinct feature is the very long spine on the anal fin.

Blackbar Soldierfish *Myripristis jacobus* Figure 17

Length 4–8" (10–20cm)

A common species, which can be distinguished at once by the prominent black bar running across the gill cover. It does not bear the characteristic pre-opercular spine of the Squirrelfishes, and has a more dumpy shape. Colour ranges from a silvery-red to dark red; background shade seems to have some bearing on the colour density.

Nearly always found in small schools of a dozen or more, fairly close to cover during the daytime. Also found under large coral overhangs and in and around old wrecks, piles and jetties. It is not a wary fish and may be approached quite easily.

Coney *Cephalopholis fulva* Figures 18, 19 and 20

Length 6–12" (15–30cm)

A widespread and common Grouper, and one which exhibits a variety of colour phases. The commonest form in shallow waters is reddish-brown above and whitish below (Figure 18). Others are reddish or dark brown all over, covered with small blue or white spots (see Figure 19). A rarer form is bright yellow all over with blue spots (Figure 20). All are distinguished by two dark spots on the caudal peduncle and two spots on the lower lip.

They are carnivorous and feed on other small fish and crustaceans. Usually seen singly or in pairs around coral heads and reef structures. They can be approached quite easily, but if frightened will back off into holes or crevices in the coral.

Three different colour phases are illustrated and the pairs of characteristic black spots are clearly shown.

Figure 18   Coney, *Cephalopholis fulva*, common colour phase

Figure 19   Coney, *Cephalopholis fulva*, red/brown phase

Figure 20   Coney, *Cephalopholis fulva*, yellow phase

Figure 21   Red Hind, *Epinephelus guttatus*

Figure 22   Rock Hind, *Epinephelus adscensionis*

Figure 23   Harlequin Bass, *Serranus tigrinus*

Red Hind *Epinephelus guttatus* Figure 21

Length 10–21″ (25–53cm)

A common small Grouper in shallow waters. Overall colouration is yellowish-white, darker above, and the whole body is densely covered with pink or red spots. Margins of soft dorsal, caudal, and anal fin are darker, and the membranes of the spiny dorsal fins are distinctively tipped in yellow. This feature and the absence of light or dark spots below the dorsal fins distinguish the species from the **Rock Hind** and **Graysby**. Found in all reef areas but particularly on rocky broken bottoms and among coral rubble. Less wary than the Rock Hind.

Rock Hind *Epinephelus adscensionis* Figure 22

Length 8–15″ (20–37cm)

A common inshore Grouper found in all reef areas and on adjacent rock and rubble bottoms. It is much more wary than the broadly similar Red Hind, particularly larger specimens. Usual body colour is pale whitish, sometimes yellowish-green, completely covered with pale brown spots. The distinctive feature is the row of large dark spots along the back below the dorsal fin, these are absent on the Red Hind.

Difficult to approach closely, and seems to be entirely bottom dwelling.

Harlequin Bass *Serranus tigrinus* Figure 23

Length 3–4″ (7.5–10cm)

A common and widespread Bass with distinctive black/brown irregular bars and blotches on a mainly yellowish-white body colour, which tends to darken to olive green on larger specimens. Usually seen singly close to the bottom in all areas around rocks, coral rubble and other forms of cover.

It is carnivorous and feeds mainly on small crustacea. It is not a wary fish and is easily approached.

Tobacco Fish *Serranus tabacarius*

Length 4–6″ (10–15cm)

A fairly common and widespread Bass, the overall colouration is orange to orange/brown with pale blotches on the back, colouration is variable however and sometimes dark blotches or pale areas surrounded by dark blotches are evident. Seen usually in small groups of 2–4 or singly. More common in 20–40 feet (6–12 metres) of water where it can be found a foot or two off the bottom around coral, rocks etc. It is more wary than *S. tigrinus* and difficult to photograph as it always presents a head-on appearance if approached too closely.

Barred Hamlet *Hypoplectrus puella* Figure 24

Length 2-5" (5-12cm)

Probably the most common Hamlet in the West Indies. Can be found in all localities, but prefers coral and coral rubble areas. It is normally seen singly and can be approached quite easily. No obvious colour or marking variations have been observed although intensity of markings does vary between individuals and the fish can take on a paler shade when passing over light sandy areas.

Yellowbellied Hamlet *Hypoplectrus aberrans* Figure 25

Length 2-4" (5-10cm)

A rather drab Hamlet which is easily mistaken for one of the adult Damselfishes. It is not uncommon in our area, but nowhere abundant. Colouration is brownish on the upper half of the body and yellow on the lower half. There is usually a dark spot on the top of the caudal peduncle behind the soft dorsal fin. Not wary and easily approached.

Shy Hamlet *Hypoplectrus guttavarius* Figure 26

Length 3-4" (7.5-10cm)

Said to be uncommon, but in the East Caribbean area it has been seen in several places in the 15-50 feet (4.5-15 metre) depth range. In some areas it is seen frequently. Colouration is dark brown above, sometimes with a bluish sheen, and bright yellow below with all fins bright yellow. All specimens observed had the large black spot on the snout rimmed in brilliant blue, and the diagonal blue stripe below the eye. Seen either singly or in pairs over reefs and around isolated coral heads. It is not a wary species and is easily approached.

Figure 24   Barred Hamlet, *Hypoplectrus puella*

Figure 25   Yellowbellied Hamlet, *Hypoplectrus aberrans*

Figure 26   Shy Hamlet, *Hypoplectrus guttavarius*

Figure 27   Glasseye, *Priacanthus cruentatus*

Figure 28   Bigeye, *Priacanthus arenatus*

Figure 29   Soapfish, *Rypticus saponaceus*

Glasseye *Priacanthus cruentatus* Figure 27

Length 6–12″ (15–30cm)

A fairly common but nowhere abundant fish. It is mainly nocturnal in habit and will be found in coral caves, and beneath deep ledges. It is particulary fond of old wrecks and other underwater structures. Colouration is variable from silvery-red to dark red, but more often silvery-red with a darker, mottled, reddish pattern.

It is carnivorous and feeds on small crustaceans, worms, and plankton. Often seen hanging motionless in the water and can be easily approached.

Bigeye *Priacanthus arenatus* Figure 28

Length 6–12″ (15–30cm)

Similar in general appearance to *P. cruentatus*, it will be found in similar localities. Colouration is less variable and is usually bright red with darker red membranes on all fins. Some specimens exhibit a pronounced lateral line marking. It is fairly common but tends to favour deeper water. Can be approached quite easily and has the same feeding habits as *P. cruentatus*.

Soapfish *Rypticus saponaceus* Figure 29

Length 6–10″ (15–25cm)

The most common Soapfish in our waters and the largest, it is a drab brownish-grey fish, with pale and rather indistinct spots on the body and dorsal fin. Fins in larger specimens blue/grey. It is a furtive-looking fish which constantly gives the impression of being terrified. It is found skulking alone around rocks and coral heads and will press itself into a corner or vanish into holes in the coral if approached too closely. Look into small caves and recesses and you will probably see this species. Soapfish are covered with a slimy mucus, presumably as a means of protection against predators.

A smaller species *R. subbifrenatus* (4–6″ or 10–15cm) is similar in general shape but with more distinct black spots on the body and fins. It is not common.

Flamefish *Apogon maculatus* Figure 30

Length 2–3″ (5–7.5cm)

A common but nocturnal Cardinalfish, which will be found in recesses and caves in all coral and rocky areas. Colouration is vivid red with a dark bar on the caudal peduncle and a large dark spot below the second dorsal fin. The most distinctive feature is the pair of brilliant silver eye stripes which separates this species from other Apogons. All have very large eyes for their size and are said to be carnivorous.

Creole Fish *Paranthias furcifer* Figure 31

Length 6–9″ (15–22.5cm)

Usually seen in small schools just above the bottom, often in the same areas as the Blue Chromis. Not uncommon but apparently not widespread in our area. Colouration of all species seen was salmon pink and the distinctive spots on the upper half of the body can be white or a darker colour. The caudal fin is deeply forked. In water deeper than 20 feet (6 metres), this fish appears pale blue in colour due to absorption of the delicate pink shade. Feeds on plankton and other waterborne organisms.

Copper Sweeper *Pempheris schomburgki* Figure 32

Length 2–4″ (5–10cm)

Also called the Glassy Sweeper. A common and very distinctive little fish, but being nocturnal will only be found during daylight hours inside caves, wrecks and other sheltered areas. Body shape is highly compressed and the overall colour ranges through a silvery-copper shade to olive green; often iridescent, depending on the viewing angle. There is a dark band at the base of the broad anal fin and the eye is large.

Most large caves and old wrecks contain schools of this species, and they are easily approached.

Figure 30   Flamefish, *Apogon maculatus*

Figure 31   Creole Fish, *Paranthias furcifer*

Figure 32   Copper Sweeper, *Pempheris schomburgki*

Figure 33   Fairy Basslet, *Gramma loreto*

Figure 34   Redspotted Hawkfish, *Ambylcirrhitus pinos*

Fairy Basslet *Gramma loreto*   Figure 33

Length 1–3″ (2.5–7.5cm)

Also called the **Royal Gramma** by fish fanciers. It is a popular aquarium fish. Generally common in our area but since it lives in and around cracks and holes in large coral heads, and in caves in the reef drop-off, a keen eye is needed to find this species. Colouration is distinctive and brilliant, the front half of the body being vivid purple and the rear half bright yellow.

Look under ledges and in recesses in large coral heads and you will find these little fishes swimming upside down. They can be observed closely and colouration seems to be identical at all stages of growth.

Redspotted Hawkfish *Amblycirrhitus pinos*   Figure 34

Length 2–3″ (5–7.5cm)

The only species of the family **Cirrhitidae** in our area. It is a distinctive and relatively common little fish which is particularly fond of old eroded reef tops, piles of coral rubble and encrusted wrecks and walls. Has not been observed free swimming. It tends to scuttle about from perch to perch and is often seen poised vertically or inverted among sponges and hydroids on encrusted wrecks and sea walls. Colouration does not change and is essentially whitish with five darker, yellowish-brown vertical bars, and a prominent dark spot at rear of soft dorsal fin. The front part of the body, head, and dorsal fin are covered with distinctive red freckles.

Thought to feed on small invertebrates, worms etc. It is probably territorial, and is always seen singly.

Figure 35   French Grunt, *Haemulon flavolineatum*

Figure 36   Smallmouth Grunt, *Haemulon chrysargyreum*

French Grunt *Haemulon flavolineatum* Figure 35

Length 6–9″ (15–22.5cm)

Certainly the most common Grunt in our area. Found in large schools where there are reefs, coral heads or rocky bottoms. Colouration is silvery with yellow striping which usually slants diagonally upwards below the lateral line and is more or less horizontal above. All fins yellowish. The decided overall yellow appearance of this species makes it easy to distinguish from the other Grunts. Juveniles are silvery, with a few brownish, horizontal stripes and a dark spot on the side of the caudal peduncle, this colouration is found on many juvenile Grunts making identification extremely difficult. Easily approached underwater.

Grunts, along with the Soldierfishes are among the first species which will colonise artificial reefs.

Smallmouth Grunt *Haemulon chrysargyreum* Figure 36

Length 4–6″ (10–15cm)

Commonly found in small schools in most areas, around coral heads, wrecks, and other underwater structures; often seen in company with the French Grunt. Colouration is distinctive, a silvery-blue/grey body with bold yellow body stripes. All fins are usually bright yellow. Will readily colonise artificial reef structures like most of the other Grunts covered here.

Figure 37   Tomtate, *Haemulon aurolineatum*

Figure 38   Black Margate, *Anisotremus surinamensis*

Tomtate *Haemulon aurolineatum* Figure 37

Length 4–8″ (10–20cm)

A small schooling Grunt, it is common in our area over sea grass meadows, coral patches and around coral heads. Body colour is silvery-grey and there are two yellow lines running laterally, the most prominent line running through the eye to the large dark blotch at the base of the caudal fin. This dark blotch is a distinguishing feature and is evident on adult fish as well as juveniles. Not wary when near cover, and easily approached.

Black Margate *Anisotremus surinamensis* Figure 38

Length 9–15″ (22.5–37.5cm)

Common in most areas over reef and rubble bottoms. It stays close to the bottom and will often be found under ledges and inside old wrecks. Colouration is distinctive, being a silvery-grey colour, with blackish fins, and a very broad black bar behind the pectoral fins extending from the lateral line down to the pelvic fins. Usually seen singly in our area, and is difficult to approach when away from cover.

Goatfishes Mullidae

Two species are found in the area. Both are common and widespread, and can be seen, often together, over areas of sand, shingle and sea grass. They are bottom feeders and are equipped with sensory barbels under the chin for locating and rooting out small invertebrates which live in and under the sand. Neither species is particularly wary and with care can be approached quite easily.

Yellow Goatfish *Mulloidichthys martinicus* Figure 39
Length 6–12" (15–30cm)

Almost always seen in schools of a dozen or more hovering one or two feet above sand and other soft bottoms. Colouration is whitish to pale yellow/green, with a distinctive yellow lateral line and tail fin. Other fins tend to pale yellow.

It appears to feed little during the daytime, but has on odd occasions been observed feeding voraciously when water visibility has been poor, and when the sea bed has been churned up.

Spotted Goatfish *Pseudupeneus maculatus* Figure 40
Length 6–10" (15–25cm)

Unlike the Yellow Goatfish, this species is often seen singly or in small groups of 4–6. It appears to be constantly rooting around in the sand for food and rarely seems to rest. The illustration shows the sensory barbels in use, and this species can often be located by the clouds of fine silt thrown up during its frantic search for food. Colouration is pale pink to pale reddish-brown with three large dark and distinctive red/brown blotches under the dorsal fin. This fish exhibits rapidly changing colour intensity, particularly of the three blotches, which can be darkened or lightened at will. When it settles on the bottom to rest, colours will darken noticeably.

Yellowhead Jawfish *Opistognathus aurifrons* Figure 41
Length 2–3" (5–7.5cm)

The most attractive of the Jawfishes, it lives in a vertical stone-lined burrow on sandy/shingle bottoms. It is carnivorous and is usually seen hovering vertically over its burrow waiting for passing zooplankton in the water. It is easily frightened and will dart tail first back into its burrow if the critical distance is transgressed. Great care and patience are needed to observe this fish in any detail. Body colour is pale blue with a distinctive yellow head and prominent eyes.

Figure 39   Yellow Goatfish, *Mulloidichthys martinicus*

Figure 40   Spotted Goatfish, *Pseudupeneus maculatus*

Figure 41   Yellowhead Jawfish, *Opistognathus aurifrons*

Figure 42   Jackknife Fish, *Equetus lanceolatus*, juvenile

Figure 43   High-hat (Cubbyu), *Equetus acuminatus*

Figure 44   Spotted Drum, *Equetus punctatus*

Jackknife Fish *Equetus lanceolatus* Figure 42

Length 3–8″ (7.5–20cm), juvenile

Widely distributed but not common in our area. It is a distinctive fish with similar colouration and markings at all stages. The juvenile illustrated can easily be confused with the juvenile Spotted Drum but does not have the black snout of that species. A popular aquarium fish it swims along near the bottom with an undulating motion and is easily approached. Found on broken and sandy bottoms around coral heads (look under ledges).

High-Hat *Equetus acuminatus* Figure 43

Length 5–8″ (12–20cm)

Also known as the **Cubbyu**, and in our area less common than the larger Spotted Drum. It is a rather retiring species and will be found near the bottom in reef areas and around rocks and coral heads. Not a wary fish but it tends to stay under ledges and inside sandy recesses. Colouration is dark brown with white lateral stripes sometimes extending through head and tail. Body markings distinguish it at once from the other Drums. Usually seen singly.

Spotted Drum *Equetus punctatus* Figure 44

Length 6–10″ (15–25cm)

Not uncommon in our area, but is usually found under ledges close to the bottom or inside small, sandy-bottomed caves. This is the largest of the Drums. Colouration is distinctive in adults with the broad black or dark brown body stripes and the white spotted dorsal and caudal fins. Juveniles are very similar to the juvenile Jackknife fish and the only obvious distinguishing feature is the black snout. Nearly always seen singly and is easily approached.

Angelfishes Pomacanthinae

Probably the most beautiful of all reef fishes. They are distinguished by deep compressed bodies, and the presence of stout pre-opercular spines. This spine is not present on the Butterflyfishes which are often included in the same family. In most species the juveniles differ greatly in colour and sometimes shape, from the adult fish. They can be found in all locations but prefer rock and reef areas. Over sand and sea grass they will tend to congregate around isolated rocks and coral heads. Usually seen singly or in pairs, they feed for the most part on algae and various sponges.

Cherubfish *Centropyge argi*   Figure 45

Length 1–2″ (2.5–5cm)

This elusive, brilliant blue, little fish bears the characteristic pre-opercular spine of all Angelfish, although at first glance it is likely to be mistaken for a species of Damselfish. It is sometimes called the Pygmy Angelfish. Not common in shallow waters. It is a rather wary fish, and its sharp, darting movements in and out of holes in rock and coral make it difficult to approach and observe closely. Smaller specimens are like brilliant blue jewels. Colouration blue, sometimes vivid, yellow/orange head and chest. There is a distinctive blue ring around the yellow eye. All fins are blue except the pectorals which are yellowish. Usually seen in pairs on reefs and around coral heads and rocks. In deeper water it is often found in small groups on the bottom, flitting in and out of coral rubble.

A related but rarer species, the Flameback Cherubfish *Centropyge aurantonotus* has been observed in our area. Colouration and size are similar but head and *back* of this species is orange to red.

Figure 45   Cherubfish, *Centropyge argi*

Figure 46   Rock Beauty, *Holacanthus tricolor*, adult

Figure 47   Queen Angelfish, *Holacanthus ciliaris*, adult

Rock Beauty *Holacanthus tricolor* Figure 46

Length 4–8″ (10–20cm)

One of the most common and easily identified of the Angelfishes. Body of adult fish is distinctly black and yellow with brilliant blue rim markings on upper and lower parts of the eye. It is fairly easy to approach and will be found over all reefs, and around coral heads and rocky areas. Seen either singly or in pairs. The juvenile is predominantly yellow with a single blue ringed black spot in the middle of the body beneath the dorsal fin. As growth progresses this spot expands, and the blue ring fades until the black area spreads out to take the form of the adult fish.

Queen Angelfish *Holacanthus ciliaris* Figure 47

Length 8–15″ (20–37.5cm)

Probably the most striking of all Caribbean Angelfishes, particularly large adult specimens. Could be confused with the Blue Angelfish, but is distinguished by a prominent blue, ringed, freckled spot or 'crown' on the forehead, and an all-yellow tail. Overall colour is blue to greenish-blue with distinctive yellow rimmed scales. Juveniles are dark brown through to dark green with three blue vertical stripes on the body and two stripes on the head, one either side of the eye. Traces of these stripes still remain on fairly large specimens.

Seen either alone or in pairs, in and around coral reefs and large isolated coral heads. It is relatively common around some of the East Caribbean islands but rare in others. Not wary and easily approached underwater.

French Angelfish *Pomacanthus paru* Figures 48 and 49

Length 12–15″ (30–37.5cm)

Seen either alone or more commonly in pairs. It is an inquisitive fish, and after initial flight will often return to watch the observer. Some specimens are exceedingly tame. Overall colour is dark brown to black with body scales rimmed in yellow. A yellow bar at the pectoral fin base distinguishes it from the similar Grey Angelfish. Tip of dorsal filament also rimmed in yellow. In almost adult fish, traces of the yellow bars found on juveniles (Figure 49) still remain and this can be seen in Figure 48. Fully adult fish do not show these bars. Juveniles are more commonly seen. They are almost black in colour, with three prominent vertical yellow bars. The tail fin is rounded, whereas the very similar juvenile Grey Angelfish has a square cut tail fin.

Blue Angelfish *Holacanthus isabelita*

Length 8–15″ (20–37.5cm)

Similar in shape and general appearance to the Queen Angelfish but without the distinctive forehead 'crown'. Overall colour is vaguely bluish-purple with light edged scales. Head and chest are distinctly deeper blue with extremities of all fins rimmed in yellow.

Juveniles are *very* similar to the Queen Angelfish young, except for the second blue stripe on the body which is straight instead of curved.

Appears to be rare in the West Indies area of the Caribbean, but said to be more common in the Bahamas and Florida.

Grey Angelfish *Pomacanthus arcuatus*

Length 10–18″ (25–45cm)

One of the largest, and in some areas, the most common Angelfish. Overall colour ranges through grey to pale brown with a light edge to the scales. Upper surface of the pectoral fins is yellow and the end of the tail fin is straight. This last feature distinguishes it at once from *P. paru* which has a rounded tail fin. Juveniles are black with yellow bars and almost identical to the juvenile *P. paru* except for the straight cut tail fin.

Seen singly or in pairs over most reef areas and around piles, jetties and old wrecks. Will sometimes be found with *P. paru*. Both these species being tame and inquisitive are unfortunately fair game for the spear-fisherman, and in many areas their numbers and distribution have been reduced considerably.

Figure 48   French Angelfish, *Pomacanthus paru*, adult

Figure 49   French Angelfish, *Pomacanthus paru*, juvenile

Figure 50   Banded Butterflyfish, *Chaetodon striatus*

Figure 51   Foureye Butterflyfish, *Chaetodon capistratus*

Banded Butterflyfish   *Chaetodon striatus*   Figure 50

Length 3–5" (7.5–12.5cm)

One of the most common of the reef Butterflyfishes. In common with the other species covered it has a highly compressed deep body. Essentially silvery-white in colour with two wide vertical black bands on the body. A thinner black bar runs through the eye, and it has black inner margins to the tail, soft dorsal and soft anal fins. Juveniles are similarly marked but also have a dark-ringed spot below the soft dorsal area.

Usually seen in pairs, or occasionally singly. It feeds on small worms, tube worms, and small crustacea. Can be approached quite easily and is found over reefs, around coral heads and frequently over sea grass beds.

Foureye Butterflyfish   *Chaetodon capistratus*   Figure 51

Length 3–5" (7.5–12.5cm)

Probably the commonest of the Caribbean Butterflyfishes and immediately recognised by the prominent, dark, ocellated spot below the soft dorsal fin. Body colour is pale grey with well defined dark diagonal lines running above and below the lateral line. Seen over all reef areas, usually in pairs it will frequently be found in the vicinity of large vase sponges.

Longsnout Butterflyfish   *Prognathodes aculeatus*

Length 2–3" (5–7.5cm)

A smaller species, and although not commonly found in shallow water, it is quite abundant on deeper offshore reefs. Colouration is yellow/orange on the upper body and whitish below. As the name suggests it has a long protruding snout which it uses for picking off small crustacea, tube worms and occasionally coral polyps. Seen singly or in pairs over offshore reefs.

Reef Butterflyfish   *Chaetodon sedenarius*

Length 3–4" (7.5–10cm)

Not common in shallow waters and nowhere abundant in our area. Colouration is mainly silvery-yellow, darker yellow on the upper half of the body, with dark margins to the soft dorsal and anal fins.

Spotfin Butterflyfish   *Chaetodon ocellatus*

Length 3–6" (7.5–15cm)

An uncommon species in our area, but one of the largest of the genus. Body colour is silvery-white with pale yellow fins. There is a large rather indistinct dark spot below the soft dorsal area and a small dark spot on the extremity of the soft dorsal.

Blue Chromis *Chromis cyanea* Figure 52

Length 2–3″ (5–7.5cm)

A brilliant blue fish which presents no problems with recognition. Found in small and large groups over offshore reefs often in company with *C. multilineata*. Prefers deeper waters, and is especially fond of beds of Staghorn Coral in the 20–50 feet (6–15 metres) depth range, but also occurs beyond 100 feet (30 metres). Feeds on passing plankton and is quite easily approached.

Yellow Edge Chromis *Chromis multilineata* Figure 53

Length 2–4″ (5–10cm)

Also called the Brown Chromis. One of the commonest of the small reef fishes, it occurs over all reef areas both shallow and deep. Found in small groups or dense aggregations of hundreds of fish. Colouration is brownish-green on the upper half of the body and paler silvery yellow/brown below. The dorsal fin is edged with yellow and there is a distinctive white spot at the end of the dorsal fin. Feeds on passing plankton. It is not a wary fish and will quite happily accept food from divers.

Sergeant Major *Abudefduf saxatilus* Figure 54

Length 4–6″ (10–15cm)

A common and striking fish which is instantly recognisable. Found in all areas over reefs and shallows but especially fond of large coral heads and sunken shallow wrecks. Occurs singly or in small groups, although juveniles may be seen in larger groups. Usual colouration is silvery-grey tending to bright yellow along the back, with five dark vertical bars. Adult males take on a dark bluish-purple colour when guarding egg patches, and are usually very aggressive at this stage. Food apparently consists of a wide variety of algae, worms, plankton and other small marine life. Being constantly on the move it is not easy to approach, and will take cover very rapidly.

Figure 52   Blue Chromis, *Chromis cyanea*

Figure 53   Yellow Edge Chromis, *Chromis multilineata*

Figure 54   Sergeant Major, *Abudefduf saxatilus*

Damselfishes Pomacentridae

The most numerous of all small reef fishes you see will almost certainly be the Damselfishes. Every section of reef and every coral head supports several species of these attractive little fishes, many of which are among the most colourful of all reef dwellers. Several species are territorial and comically aggressive, especially when guarding their eggs. All are busy little fish, constantly darting in and out of holes and crevices in the coral; and for this reason and their small size, are very difficult to photograph successfully.

Identification of large adults can be very confusing as several species take on a dark brown colouration with few distinguishing marks. Juveniles invariably differ greatly in colouration and marking from adult fish.

Food consists of a wide range of algae and other plant food, small anemones, worms and crustacea; in fact, almost anything small enough to be consumed.

Cocoa Damselfish *Eupomacentrus variabilis*

Length 2–4″ (5–10cm)

A small and common Damselfish which is easily confused with the Beaugregory or the Honey Damselfish. Adults assume a dusky brown colour like several other species of Damselfish and are extremely difficult to separate underwater. Colouration of juveniles and intermediate fish, yellow with a blue dorsal and blue wash on head and back. The dorsal surface and head covered with lighter blue spots and streaks. There is a large black spot on the dorsal fin and a smaller black spot on the caudal peduncle. Found in all inshore shallows over reefs, coral rubble and other rocky areas, sometimes in only a foot or two of water.

Bicolor Damselfish *Eupomacentrus partitus*

Length 2–3″ (5–7.5cm)

Easily identified, the front half of body and head is dusky brown and sharply divided from the rear half which ranges from orange/yellow to silvery-grey. Juveniles are also bicoloured and apart from subtle variations in colouration the fish is easily recognisable, being bicoloured at all stages. This is a common and widespread species, found in all reef and rocky areas.

Dusky Damselfish   *Eupomacentrus dorsopunicans*

Length 2–5″ (5–12.5cm)

A common species found on all reefs and rocky bottoms, the adult fish is dusky brownish-grey in colour, or sometimes black with faint blue freckles on the head and chest. Can be confused with other adult Damsels. Juveniles are lighter in shade with a red/orange stripe running from the mouth along the back to the soft dorsal, a blue-ringed, black spot on caudal peduncle and a larger blue-ringed spot below the dorsal fin. Can be easily approached but like other Damselfishes is constantly on the move.

Yellowtail Damselfish   *Microspathodon chrysurus*   Fig 55

Length 3–4″ (7.5–10cm)

A very common Damselfish over all reef areas which presents no identification problem. Overall colour is dusky brown in adults with a distinctive yellow/yellow-brown tail fin. The head and upper half of body bears distinctive small blue spots. Juveniles are also distinctive being a dull blue with myriads of brilliant lighter blue spots over the whole body. They are frequently found in and around Fire Corals.

Figure 55   Yellowtail Damselfish, *Microspathodon chrysurus*

Figure 56   Honey Damselfish, *Eupomacentrus mellis*

Figure 57   Yellow Damselfish (Threespot Damselfish), *Eupomacentrus planifrons*, juvenile

Honey Damselfish *Eupomacentrus mellis* Figure 56

Length 1.5–2″ (3.5–5cm)

Relatively common in our area, sometimes in only a few feet of water. Found around coral heads, eroded reefs and coral rubble. Can be confused with the juvenile Beaugregory and Cocoa Damselfish, but it does not have the dark spot on the tail base and there is no blue background colour underneath the blue spots and streaks on head and back. Constantly on the move, flitting in and out of crevices it is difficult to observe closely.

Yellow Damselfish *Eupomacentrus planifrons* Figure 57

Length 2–4″ (5–10cm)

Adults are dusky brown in colour with yellowish fins. There is a black spot at the root of the pectoral fin which is rather indistinct. Juveniles are more distinctive, being bright yellow with a more obvious black spot at root of the pectorals, a large black spot on the caudal peduncle and a blue-ringed, black spot below the dorsal fin. Common and widespread on all reefs. Sometimes called Threespot Damsel, presumably from markings on the juveniles.

Wrasses Labridae

Wrasses form one of the largest fish families in all temperate and tropical waters, and are distributed widely. All are carnivorous, and often brightly coloured. Identification can be difficult, as most juveniles differ greatly from adult fish, and several adult species exhibit varying colour phases. Male adults are often very different in colouration and size from females, and some species have the ability to change sex during adult life. Generally speaking the males are more gaudily coloured, and larger than the females.

Spanish Hogfish *Bodianus rufus*

Length 4–15″ (10–37.5cm)

A fairly common species around reefs and coral heads. Colouration is essentially blue on the upper frontal half of the body and front part of dorsal fin, and yellow/pale orange below. All fins and tail are yellow, including the posterior part of the dorsal fin. Juveniles have virtually the same colour pattern, and the species presents no problems with recognition. Feeds on crustacea, sea urchins and other invertebrates. Large specimens tend to be rather wary and will back off into crevices in coral heads if approached too closely.

Creole Wrasse *Clepticus parrae*   Figure 58

Length 4–10″ (10–25cm)

A very common Wrasse of the offshore reef areas, but not normally seen in inshore shallows. It swims in schools, sometimes large, either in mid-water or close to the bottom. When viewed in deep water it appears totally blue, but is in fact bluish-purple with subtle green/yellow and red indistinct blotches around the caudal peduncle and anal areas. The top of the head and mouth areas are a much darker blue, and almost black in large specimens. Juveniles are an overall pale blue in colour with darker vertical bars above the lateral line.

It is a fairly wary fish and is constantly on the move. Often seen near the bottom in company with the Blue Chromis.

Figure 58   Creole Wrasse, *Clepticus parrae*

Figure 59   Yellowhead Wrasse, *Halichoeres garnoti*

Figure 60   Puddingwife, *Halichoeres radiatus*, intermediate stage

Yellowhead Wrasse *Halichoeres garnoti*   Figure 59

Length 3–6″ (7.5–15cm)

A common species, particularly around coral heads, coral rubble and old wrecks. Juveniles are bright yellow with a prominent blue lateral line from eye to tail and are seen in small groups. Intermediate fish tend to be dark orange above and whitish below with two dark eye stripes. Adults develop the characteristic inverted 'L' shape black stripe and black tail. The head and front part of body are yellowish and greenish inside the dark stripe.

Both juveniles and adults are continually on the move, but a good way to attract them is to break open a sea urchin.

Puddingwife *Halichoeres radiatus*   Figure 60

Length 4–12″ (10–30cm)

This is the largest of the genus, and extremely variable in colouration and markings. The illustration shows an intermediate fish and the large dark blotch halfway along the dorsal fin and the five faint vertical white body bars are evident at most stages. The blue/green spots and scrawls vary in intensity on adults and intermediate fish. Juveniles are totally different, having two yellow/orange broad stripes along the body but still with one or two dark blotches on the dorsal fin and the five broad white vertical bars on the upper body. It is relatively common in all reef areas, and very fond of wrecks and other underwater structures.

Clown Wrasse *Halichoeres maculipinna* Figure 61

Length 2–5″ (5–12.5cm)

One of the commonest small Wrasses in all shallow water reef areas. They are voracious feeders, and will appear from nowhere if you break up a few sea urchins. Colouration is variable and juveniles are different again. Distinctive features are the red line patterns on the head and normally a large dark spot on the spinous portion of the dorsal fin. Usual overall colouration of adult males is greenish above and pale pink to white below. Juveniles are generally black on the upper half with a yellow band above, and whitish below, again with a dark spot on the dorsal fin.

Bluehead Wrasse *Thalassoma bifasciatum* Figure 62

Length 3–6″ (7.5–15cm)

A common species, frequently found in same areas as *H. garnoti*. The blue phase adult male is quite distinctive with a blue head and front half divided by two prominent vertical black bars which are interspersed with a white/ pale blue broader bar. The rear half of the body is greenish-blue. Other males, females and juveniles tend to be yellow with a black/brown lateral stripe and a black spot at the front of the dorsal fin. As growth progresses, the black lateral stripe breaks down into dark blotches. These yellow and brownish colour phases are more commonly found.

Slippery Dick *Halichoeres bivittatus* Figure 63

Length 3–6″ (7.5–15cm)

Probably the commonest of the Wrasses in our area, it is found over all shallow reefs, and adjacent rubble flats. Colouration is again variable, but the principal features are the two dark body stripes on a whitish body and the characteristic red markings on the head and caudal fins.

They are rapidly attracted by breaking up a sea urchin, and are constantly on the move.

Figure 61   Clown Wrasse, *Halichoeres maculipinna*

Figure 62   Bluehead Wrasse, *Thalassoma bifasciatum*, adult male

Figure 63   Slippery Dick, *Halichoeres bivittatus*

Figure 64   Stoplight Parrotfish, *Sparisoma viride*, female

Figure 65   Stoplight Parrotfish, *Sparisoma viride*, male

Stoplight Parrotfish *Sparisoma viride* Figures 64 and 65

Length 12–20" (30–50cm) male   Length 10–18" (25–45cm) female

This is one of the commonest Parrotfishes in our area and one of the most attractive. Colouration of males and females differs widely as can be seen in the plates. The species is particularly common over Staghorn Coral beds, but is widespread over all reef areas.

Colouration of adult males is essentially bluish-green with a bright yellow spot near upper edge of the gill cover; three diagonal stripes on the upper half of the head and a yellowish blotch on the tail fin. Adult females are dark reddish-brown on the upper half of the body and a brighter red below. The only feature marks are silvery-white individual scales on some larger females.

The Parrotfishes are herbivorous and feed on algae and other plant food, which is scraped from coral and rock with their strong parrot-like teeth. This feeding process (which is quite audible underwater), results in severe damage to corals, as a great deal of coral is ingested along with their food, ground up, and later excreted.

All Parrotfish rest on the bottom at night, often wedged between rocks. Some species will cocoon themselves in a thin mucous membrane while sleeping.

Striped or Mottlefin Parrotfish   *Scarus croicensis*   Fig 66

Length 6–10″ (15–25cm)

A common species in our area, and found over all reefs and adjacent rocky areas. Often confused with *S. taeniopterus* but adult males of these two species do have distinguishing features. The upper blue eye stripe is more or less continuous over the eye and the reddish band on the dorsal fin has a broken or mottled appearance. The caudal fin has blue margins. Females and juveniles are very similar to *S. taeniopterus* and are not readily separated during underwater observation.

Princess Parrotfish   *Scarus taeniopterus*   Figure 67

Length 8–12″ (20–30cm) male   Length 7–11″ (17.5–27.5cm) female

A relatively common species over all inshore and offshore reef areas, but one that is often confused with the Striped or Mottlefin Parrotfish, *S. croicensis*. Females and juveniles of the two species are drab, brown-striped fishes and difficult to separate. Adult males do differ in several respects however.

The tail fin of the Princess Parrotfish has reddish margins, the red central band of the dorsal fin is solid and not mottled, and the upper blue eyestripe is broken by the eye. There is also a large yellowish blotch to the rear of the pectoral fins.

Redband Parrotfish   *Sparisoma aurofrenatum*   Figure 68

Length 7–10″ (17.5–25cm) male   Length 6–10″ (15–25cm) female

A fairly common species which is widespread over all reef and rock areas. Adult males are essentially bluish-green with reddish-brown dorsal and anal fins. A distinctive yellow spot containing one or two black freckles is found above the pectoral fins, and a red/orange line runs diagonally from corner of mouth, to below the eye. Females are dark brownish-red or greenish-red above and light red below, with a very distinctive white spot on the caudal peduncle. Feeds on algae and other plant food which is scraped from corals and rocks.

Figure 66   Striped Parrotfish, *Scarus croicensis*, male

Figure 67   Princess Parrotfish, *Scarus taeniopterus*, male

Figure 68   Redband Parrotfish, *Sparisoma aurofrenatum*

Figure 69   Queen Triggerfish, *Balistes vetula*

Queen Triggerfish   *Balistes vetula*   Figure 69

Length 6–15" (15–37.5cm)

Commonly called 'old wife' in the West Indies, the Queen Triggerfish is the most common species in shallow waters and certainly the most spectacular. Body shape is unmistakeable and quite highly compressed. Colouration is blue/green on upper half of body and orange/yellow on lower half. Two broad blue stripes run diagonally from the mouth and snout to below the pectoral fins. Density of colour can be changed at will, the fish going from a brilliant colour phase to a paler drab phase sometimes in a matter of seconds. Adult fish are usually found singly or in twos and threes over a wide variety of bottom terrain, from the reef itself to areas of sand and sea grass. Juveniles are often found in large numbers over sea grass beds and around small coral heads. Food consists of a variety of invertebrates, but especially sea urchins. They have small but powerful jaws and adult fish are capable of biting severely if handled carelessly.

If alarmed, Triggerfish will often worm into extremely small cracks and crevices in the coral and wedge themselves in position by means of the first dorsal spine, this is locked in position by the second spine or 'trigger'.

Blue Tang   *Acanthurus coeruleus*   Figure 70

Length 2–3″ (5–7.5cm) juvenile   Length 4–8″ (10–20cm) adult

This species is easily distinguished from *A. bahianus* and *A. chirirgus*. Adults are more highly compressed, and vary in colour from bright blue/purple to purplish-grey. The caudal 'scalpel' has a white sheath and is very prominent. Body, anal, and dorsal fins are covered with dark blue to brown horizontal lines. Juvenile fish are bright yellow and unmistakeable. Young adults will often show an indistinct yellow body overlaid with dark horizontal lines and blue fins.

It is herbivorous and will be found in the same areas as the other Surgeonfishes. In our area it is more likely to be seen singly or in small groups rather than in large schools.

Ocean Surgeon   *Acanthurus bahianus*   Figure 71

Length 6–10″ (15–25cm)

Both this species and *A. chirurgus* are widespread and common over reefs and inshore shallows. It can easily be confused with *A. chirurgus* but has a more sharply forked tail and does *not* exhibit the pale vertical body bars seen on the latter species. Frequent habitats are sea grass meadows and fairly flat shallow sandy areas with small coral heads, rubble and seaweeds. They are herbivorous and feed on sea grasses and various forms of algae.

The distinctive feature of all Surgeonfishes is the sharp 'scalpel' situated on the caudal peduncle, and severe lacerations can result if these fishes are handled carelessly. Colouration varies between pale brownish-grey to pale bluish-grey and appears to be variable. Adults are generally darker than juveniles. Dorsal and anal fins are darker and can be quite blue in some individuals. Seen in small to large groups, close to the bottom, sometimes in only one or two feet of water. Constantly on the move, it is a difficult fish to approach closely.

Doctorfish   *Acanthurus chirurgus*

Length 6–10″ (15–25cm)

Often found with *A. bahianus* and is similar in general appearance. It does, however, exhibit vertical dark body bars which may vary from very indistinct to prominent. The tail fin tips are more rounded than *A. bahianus*. Found in the same areas grazing on sea-grasses and various algae. Colouration from pale to dark greyish-brown, with darker brown dorsal and anal fins. Juveniles are paler in colour and difficult to tell apart from juveniles of *A. bahianus*.

Figure 70   Blue Tang, *Acanthurus coeruleus*, juvenile

Figure 71   Ocean Surgeon, *Acanthurus bahianus*

Figure 72 Slender Filefish, *Monacanthus tuckeri*

Figure 73 Smooth Trunkfish, *Lactophrys triqueter*

76

Slender Filefish   *Monacanthus tuckeri*   Figure 72

Length 2–3″ (5–7.5cm)

This small Filefish will often be found drifting around on coral rubble and sand bottoms, among sponges and gorgonians. Often seen in pairs, they blend in well with the background. Colouration brownish-yellow with a whitish reticulated pattern, but variable to suit the background shade. The illustration shows the characteristic 'head down' pose usually adopted.

Smooth Trunkfish   *Lactophrys triqueter*   Figure 73

Length 4–6″ (10–15cm)

The smallest and probably most common species in our area. In common with all Trunkfishes it has a rigid exoskeleton made up of bony plates, and when viewed head-on is triangular in appearance. It is a slow swimmer and propels itself by a sculling motion with all fins. Found usually in pairs in fairly shallow water over sea grass, coral rubble, and around coral heads.

Colouration is essentially dark brown to black with white spots. Feeds on small invertebrates, worms and crustacea and will often blow jets of water into soft sand to expose its prey. Easily approached and less apt to take cover than other trunkfishes.

Spotted Trunkfish   *Lactophrys bicaudalis*

Length 4–12″ (10–30cm)

A relatively common Trunkfish found in all reef areas and most adjacent sea-grass meadows. Less common than *L. triqueter*, but usually larger, and distinguished by its more rounded white snout and the three large white spots or blotches on top of the body behind the eye. Overall colour is whitish and the body is completely covered with small dark spots. It does not bear the characteristic honeycomb markings usually seen on *L. triqueter* and is not as easily approached as that species. Feeds on algae, seagrass and small crustacea.

Like all Trunkfish this species can secrete a toxic substance lethal to other fishes, and it should not be kept in an aquarium with other fishes.

Honeycomb Cowfish   *Acanthostracion polygonius*

Length 8–15″ (20–37.5cm)

Not common in shallow waters, but more frequently seen by divers in the 40–100 feet (12–30 metres) depth range on reef slopes. It is quite distinctive, with its two horns forward of the eyes, and the very obvious honeycomb markings on the pale yellow/brown body. Found close to cover or under ledges and in caves. Not particularly wary.

Spiny Puffer *Diodon holacanthus* Figure 74

Length 6–12″ (15–30cm)

Sometimes called Porcupinefish or Balloonfish because of their bizarre ability to inflate themselves in the water when threatened, and the fact that they are covered with long rigid spines which are erected with inflation. It is a weak swimmer and can be found in all areas, but especially sea grass beds and in areas with large sponge and soft coral colonies. It has strong beak-like jaws and feeds on small crabs, sea urchins and other invertebrates. Colouration is mainly light brown along the back and whitish below, the spines are whitish and normally lie flat along the body. The eyes are prominent with a yellow iris and blue/green pupil.

If caught by hand it will invariably inflate itself in the water.

Web Burrfish *Chilomycterus antillarum* Figure 75

Length 6–9″ (15–22.5cm)

Similar at first glance to the Spiny Puffer, but is distinguished from that species by the reticulated body markings, frequently hexagonal in shape, and the large dark ocellated spots. There is a large spot above the pectoral fin and a smaller one behind and below. A further large spot is found at the base of the small dorsal fin. The short spines on this species are fixed and permanently erect. Quite a common species over all reef areas, once spotted is easily approached and can be caught by hand.

Sharpnose Puffer *Canthigaster rostrata*

Length 2–4″ (5–10cm)

A very common little Puffer, which is widespread over sand and sea grass areas and around coral heads and rocks. Not so common on deeper offshore reefs. Usually seen in pairs it is easily approached and observed.

Colour is brownish-grey, lighter below with faint blue spots. Thin blue lines radiate from the eye, and around the mouth. Often swims along vertically or at an angle.

Bandtail Puffer *Sphaeroides spengleri*

Length 4–6″ (10–15cm)

Less common than *C. rostrata* it can be found in similar areas, particularly over coral rubble. Seen singly or in pairs it feeds on sea grasses, algae, and a variety of small worms and crustacea. Colouration is distinctive, greenish-brown on the back and whitish below with a row of very obvious large dark spots from head to tail. Body texture is smooth and it has the facility to inflate itself at the approach of danger.

Figure 74   Spiny Puffer, *Diodon holacanthus*

Figure 75   Web Burrfish, *Chilomycterus antillarum*

Figure 76   Spotted Scorpionfish, *Scorpaena plumieri*

Figure 77   Redlip Blenny, *Ophioblennius atlanticus*

Spotted Scorpionfish *Scorpaena plumieri* Figure 76
Length 8–15″ (20–37.5cm)

This is the largest, and probably most common of our Scorpionfishes. In some areas it is abundant, especially around wrecks, coral rubble and on eroded reef tops, where it lies motionless awaiting its prey. Colouration is extremely variable, and changeable to suit the background shade.

A master of camouflage it is difficult to see, but will often give away its position by eye movements. Can be easily approached and while not aggressive, will often spread its pectoral fins as a warning. These fins are distinctive, with red to black and white bars and spots. All Scorpionfishes are well-endowed with poisonous spines on the head and the pre-operculer margin. While not considered lethal, any stings from these fishes should be taken seriously and prompt medical attention obtained. The author has on two occasions placed a gloved hand on this species in mistake for a piece of rock while taking photographs. No stings resulted, but it is debateable who reacted more violently.

A carnivorous fish with a large head and mouth, it feeds on other fishes and crustacea.

Redlip Blenny *Ophioblennius atlanticus* Figure 77
Length 2–3″ (5–7.5cm)

This species is included because it is one of the most common of the Blennies and also one of the most interesting. Body colour varies from grey to dark brown. Lips and dorsal fin are rimmed in bright orange/red. It is to be found in all reef areas, and seems to be particularly fond of old eroded reef tops and coral heads, where it will be found perched on top of coral protuberances. Appears to feed mainly on algae. When approached too closely it will dart off into a recess in the coral and then reappear a few minutes later. On some very shallow reef tops close inspection will reveal dozens of these little Blennies and they make an easy subject to study for the patient snorkeller.

Flying Gurnard *Dactylopterus volitans* Figure 78

Length 6–15" (15–37.5cm)

This strange looking fish is quite unmistakeable. A common inhabitant of sand flats and sea grass meadows, it is a bottom dwelling species and will be seen either at rest or swimming along slowly in search of small crustacea on which it feeds. The distinctive feature is the long trailing pectoral fins shown in the normal closed position in the illustration. If alarmed these pectorals are spread into large 'wings' which are spotted and fringed in brilliant blue. Overall colouration is yellow/brown to grey covered with whitish spots and blotches.

Seen singly or in small groups mainly in sea grass beds, and in places is abundant. Can be approached quite easily, but will invariably spread its large pectorals and 'glide' off.

Shortnose Batfish *Ogcocephalus nasutus* Figure 79

Length 10–12" (25–30cm)

A bizarre bottom dwelling fish, it is not uncommon, and careful searching will reveal it on soft silt and sand bottoms, and in sea grass beds. Body colour is in varying shades of brown, underside of body lighter, sometimes pinkish-red. Colouration can be lightened or darkened to suit bottom colour. It has no scales, the body being of a rough skin-like texture covered with warts or tubercles. Pectoral fins are prominent on an extended 'elbow' and are used by the fish to raise and lower its body and to propel itself along the bottom. Being a slow swimmer it is easily approached and can be caught by hand.

Feeds on small crustacea, worms and small fish which it is thought to attract by means of an appendage or bait protruding from below the long bulbous snout. A solitary fish which has only been observed singly.

Longlure Frogfish *Antennarius multiocellatus*

Length 3–6" (7.5–15cm)

One of several species of Frogfish. All are bizarre carnivorous fishes relying on camouflage, stealth and the anatomical 'lure' protruding from the snout to attract their prey.

They are not uncommon in places, but because they are generally motionless and blend in well with the background, they are extremely difficult to see. Look on sponge-encrusted walls, old wrecks, and on grass-covered rocky bottoms. Colouration is largely influenced by the terrain but is generally drab yellow to yellow/green. The ocellated dark spots are distinctive, particularly the three smaller ones on the tail.

Figure 78   Flying Gurnard, *Dactylopterus volitans*

Figure 79   Shortnose Batfish, *Ogcocephalus nasutus*

Underwater Photography

It is encouraging to see more and more underwater swimming enthusiasts forsaking their spearguns in favour of the camera. The growth of this rewarding interest has been remarkable over the past few years, and what was once a hobby of the wealthy or adventurous can now be practised by anyone prepared to learn a few basic skills.

A wide choice of underwater photographic equipment is available, and apart from offering a fascinating extra interest to the diver, good underwater photographs can be of great value to the scientist and student of marine life. Our knowledge is still very limited in this area, and while much can be learned from studies of collected specimens and creatures confined in aquaria, nothing can quite replace the value of studies made in the creatures' natural environment. Underwater photography provides a permanent and valuable record of species and their habitats.

This short chapter is intended to give the would-be underwater photographer an introduction to equipment and techniques. It is not a step by step guide, but a series of brief discussions based on the author's own experience. Several books devoted entirely to the subject are readily available and will give the reader more detailed information, but being a relatively new field, there are few hard and fast rules. The newcomer is urged to experiment as much as possible, and to keep detailed records. Experience is the best teacher, and this particularly applies to underwater photography.

The photographic illustrations in this book were all taken underwater and are a record of fishes in their natural environment. Most have been taken at close range (12–36″ or 30–90cm) because of the small size of most fishes described in this guide, and also to overcome frequent problems of poor visibility.

Contrary to popular opinion, tropical waters are not always 'gin clear', and visibility can at times be very poor indeed, particularly on coastal fringing reefs where harbours, creeks and river outlets bring down considerable volumes of sediment.

The camera used for the majority of the photographs was a **Rolleiflex 3.5F**, with or without close-up lenses, housed in various perspex underwater cases which the author designed and constructed. Depths varied from 10–140 feet (3–40 metres) and in the majority of cases suitably filtered electronic flash was used to obtain close to authentic colour.

Cameras for underwater use

A reasonable choice is available, and one can either buy a camera such as the 35 mm Nikonos which has been especially designed for underwater use and has the advantages of simplicity and compactness, or one of the custom-made underwater housings which will accept a wide range of cameras, in particular the popular 35 mm single lens reflex.

When considering the pros and cons of various outfits for underwater use, the depth of one's pocket has a considerable influence on the final choice. Any camera is capable of producing an underwater photograph if suitably housed; even the simple box camera or the Instamatic type is capable of producing acceptable results when used in clear and shallow waters.

Reflex cameras, either single or twin lens, are ideal for underwater work, and when fitted in a well-designed housing with all necessary controls, are capable of covering virtually all underwater assignments.

The facility afforded by a focussing screen confers a great advantage over those types where distances must be measured or estimated with consequent risk of error.

Many keen diver-photographers make underwater housings to suit their own cameras; this is well within the capability of the average handyman. Acrylic plastic ('Perspex') $\frac{1}{2} - \frac{5}{8}''$ (12–22mm) thick is probably the most suitable material available. It is easily worked with normal wood and metal working tools and, being transparent, enables all controls and camera settings to be seen at a glance. Wood, fibreglass, brass and aluminium are also commonly used and can all be employed in a satisfactory homemade housing. All one needs is patience and ingenuity, and a modicum of skill.

Problems and phenomena of underwater photography

Photographs taken in apparently crystal clear tropical water sometimes appear foggy. This effect is caused by myriads of tiny suspended particles in the water, and reflection and scatter of sunlight by these particles causes very low contrast.

While visual visibility can sometimes reach 100 feet (30 metres), one is limited to photographic distances of only 20 feet (6 metres) or so, even in these ideal conditions, again because of the low contrast of the whole scene.

Generally speaking, visibility of 40–50 feet (12–15 metres) is considered good for photography and will enable reasonably clear shots to be taken of anything up to 10 feet (3 metres) away.

Even in dirty water it is still possible to obtain successful close-up photographs if care is taken with lighting. Adapt your technique to the prevailing conditions and you will be pleasantly surprised at the success rate achieved.

Distances underwater are not what they appear. Because refraction of light rays occurs between water and the air inside a camera case, all underwater objects appear to be one third larger, or closer, than they really are. You cannot therefore measure say 3 feet (a metre) to an object and transfer this to your camera focussing scale; the object will not be in focus. The camera will see things as you do, and failing a reflex system which will always focus correctly, it is best to estimate distances and transfer the estimate to your camera focussing scale. If you wish to be precise, calibrate a measuring stick, making every 3 inch (7.5 centimetre) marking 4 inches (10 centimetres) long and transfer this reading to your camera, i.e. every 4 inches (10 centimetres) of actual distance = 3 inches (7.5 centimetres) on your camera focussing scale. These comments only apply to lenses mounted behind *flat* portholes.

Needless to say, fish do not take kindly to being prodded with a measuring stick and are unlikely to stay around while you make ready to photograph them. This technique is, however, extremely helpful for photographing inanimate objects or stationary creatures such as starfish, anemones and corals. Wire frames and all sorts of ingenious devices have been used to overcome focussing problems with non-reflex cameras, but reflex focussing does offer considerable advantages, especially for moving objects.

Low contrast is a major problem with monochrome photography, but can be improved by the use of yellow filters, or preferably extended development of the film.

With colour photography there is a far more acute problem, namely loss of colour with increasing depth and/or distance. Unfortunately, water is a very effective and somewhat selective filter of light rays. Colours at the long end of the spectrum are the first to be affected and for all practical purposes reds are effectively absorbed through a water path of 10–15 feet (3–4.5 metres). Oranges are next to go, followed by yellows, until at 40 feet (12 metres) or so the colour film is incapable of recording any colour other than a predominant blue or blue/green effect. This can at times give very pleasing results, and will convey the underwater scene roughly as you, the diver, see it, but it is unacceptable as an accurate colour record.

Colour-compensating filters (CCR series) can be used to put back some of the missing reds, but are only partially effective and cannot be used successfully below 20 feet (6 metres) or so. Beyond this depth you have no alternative but to use artificial illumination if colours are to be recorded accurately; either flash bulbs, electronic flash or possibly continuous lighting if making cine films.

Techniques

While much useful work can be accomplished by the snorkel diver equipped with only mask, snorkel and fins, the advantages conferred by the use of an aqualung are obvious. It is, however, essential that you have been fully trained in the use of this equipment and that its use has become second nature.

Although tropical waters are warm (23–28 °C), some form of protective clothing is advisable for the underwater photographer to provide a barrier against stinging plankton, corals, jellyfish, and other sometimes invisible small creatures which have a habit of picking on the underwater cameraman. A light pair of gloves (household rubber gloves will do) are virtually essential as one is always grasping pieces of coral and rock to steady one's aim, and cuts can result to the unprotected hand. There are other more dangerous and poisonous creatures to be aware of, particularly the almost invisible Scorpionfishes, and care should be taken when approaching Stingrays and Moray eels. Treatment of minor and more serious wounds is covered elsewhere in this book.

Once you have spotted a subject to photograph, your approach should be leisurely and quiet. If it is a fish, dive down to the creature's own level and approach as slowly as possible. It is an advantage to be slightly over-weighted if any water movement is evident, as this will give better stability. During the approach, estimate the size of your subject and pre-set the focussing scale on your camera to give the desired degree of reproduction. Other controls should also be pre-set, i.e. aperture and speed. Having done this, you can approach your subject slowly with one eye pressed to the focussing screen or finder, until hopefully the subject is in focus and per-fectly framed, and you can trigger the shutter. This ideal situation rarely happens in practice and much time and wasted film is often incurred before an acceptable picture is obtained. If photographing by available light, an exposure meter will give reliable results. A selenium meter is to be pre-ferred, although less sensitive, as some CdS meters are rather colour-selective and can at times give false readings, particularly in deeper waters.

If using flash, it is advisable to carry out a series of experiments and establish your own set of guide numbers for the unit in use. As an approxi-mate guide, you will need to divide the surface guide number by 3 or 4. Positioning of the flash gun is also important, and if possible should not be mounted 'on camera' or in the same housing as the camera. Direct frontal lighting is to be avoided as an unpleasant 'snowstorm' effect can result due to reflection of light from particles suspended in the water. This effect is difficult to avoid entirely, but can be reduced if the flash head is set above and possibly to one side of the camera.

When photographing in close-up, which is necessary for single speci-mens of most reef fishes, the problem is not so acute and successful pictures can be obtained in water of very low visibility.

Opinions vary as to whether to use flash as a fill-in light to bring out the colours of the main object and allow the natural blue or blue/green colour to form a background, or whether to use it as the sole source of illumination.

Certainly, in deep waters one has to rely on flash as the sole source of illumination and tolerate an inky black background.

Where sufficient natural lighting is available, I prefer to use flash as a fill-in light, selecting an aperture/shutter speed combination to allow full illumination of the main subject only, and yet allow sufficient exposure to give some natural background detail. When working at close range, i.e. less than 3 feet (one metre), flash will normally provide the whole illumination. Cameras fitted with focal plane shutters can present problems in shallow well-lit waters, especially with electronic flash where synchronisation is limited to 1/40 or 1/60 second. In certain conditions where the subject is moving, double images can result, the main image from the flash illumination and a faint secondary image from the natural light exposure. This is not a serious or frequent problem, however, and is one that can be largely eliminated if the camera is synchronised at 1/125 second, at this speed all but the most rapid movement is arrested and sufficient exposure can be given in average depths to provide some background detail.

Almost any film can be used underwater, but as each has its own characteristics it is advisable to experiment with a range of types.

In clear, sunlit waters or with flash, I would suggest starting with one of the medium speed monochrome films (50–200 ASA). They have adequate speed and offer inherently higher contrast and finer grain than the faster films. If conditions are poor, try a medium fast film of around 400 ASA. A yellow filter can be used to advantage to improve the poor contrast usually encountered, or extended development times can also be used to the same effect, without the loss of film speed that occurs when filters are used. Using a few rolls of film on a trial and error basis, and keeping accurate records of the results, is the best recipe for success. Once you have established a suitable film/exposure/development combination, stick to it.

Regarding colour film, one has the choice of colour negative material which will produce prints, or colour transparency material which can produce both transparencies and prints. For preference, I use medium-speed transparency material (50–64 ASA) for most of my work, particularly as good quality prints can now be obtained from colour transparencies, giving one the best of both worlds.

For artificial illumination, either flash bulbs or electronic flash can be used. As a very general rule, blue bulbs should be used for distances up to 3 feet (one metre) and clear bulbs beyond that. Electronic flash will often need some form of 'warming up' filtration, colour temperature varies somewhat from unit to unit and only trial and error will decide what filtration, if any, is needed.

For very close distances, 1–2 feet (30–60 centimetres) the colour rendering may be acceptable, needing perhaps a light red filter for shots in the 2–4 feet (60–120 centimetres) range. The colour film in use will also be a contributing factor, some being 'warmer' than others.

Undoubtedly, electronic flash is the more convenient form of lighting, and is cheaper in the long run. It does, however, require a pressure-proof housing of its own, and reliable waterproof connections from unit to camera. For close-up work, there is a bewildering choice of small electronic flash units which are relatively easy to house, and provide sufficient light output for successful photographs at distances of up to 3 feet (90 centimetres) or 4 feet (120 centimetres).

If this brief introduction has given you the urge to try underwater photography, it will have accomplished its purpose. With increasing plundering and pollution of the world's oceans, you may one day find yourself with a photograph of a species that has gone the way of the Dodo.

Photographic data on illustrations in this guide

Camera   Rolleiflex 3.5f 75mm Planar lens

Housings   Own design and construction in perspex/fibreglass

Accessories   Nos. 1, 2, and 3 Rolleinar close-up lenses

Filters   Rollei R1 or R5 colour correction

Films   Kodak Ektachrome X 64 ASA and Ektachrome ER64

Lighting   Electronic flash

Depth Range   10–140 feet (3–40 metres)

Exposures   Mostly 1/125 sec: f5.6–f16

Distance Range   12–48″ (30–120cm)

Index

Angelfishes, 48
Balloonfish, 78, 79
Banded Butterflyfish, 54, 55
Bandtail Pufferfish, 78
Barred Hamlet, 32, 33
Bicolor Damselfish, 58
Bigeye, 34, 35
Black Margate, 42, 43
Blackbar Soldierfish, 26, 27
Blue Angelfish, 52
Blue Chromis, 56, 57
Blue Tang, 74, 75
Bluehead Wrasse, 66, 67
Brown Chromis, 56, 57

Cherubfish, 48, 49
Clown Wrasse, 66, 67
Cocoa Damselfish, 58
Coney, 28, 29
Copper Sweeper, 36, 37
Creole Fish, 36, 37
Creole Wrasse, 62, 63
Cubbyu, 46, 47

Damselfishes, 58
Doctorfish, 74
Dusky Damselfish, 59
Dusky Squirrelfish, 27

Fairy Basslet, 38, 39
Flamefish, 36, 37
Flying Gurnard, 82, 83
Foureye Butterflyfish, 54, 55
French Angelfish, 52, 53

French Grunt, 40, 41

Glasseye, 34, 35
Goldentail Moray, 20, 21
Goldspotted Snake Eel, 20, 21
Green Moray, 20
Grey Angelfish, 52

Harlequin Bass, 30, 31
High-Hat, 46, 47
Honey Damselfish, 60, 61
Honeycomb Cowfish, 77

Jackknife Fish, 46, 47

Lizardfish, 24, 25
Longjaw Squirrelfish, 24, 25
Longlure Frogfish, 82
Longsnout Butterflyfish, 55
Longspine Squirrelfish, 26, 27

Mottlefin Parrotfish, 70, 71

Ocean Surgeonfish, 74, 75

Peacock Flounder, 22, 23
Princess Parrotfish, 70, 71
Puddingwife, 64, 65
Pygmy Angelfish, 48, 49

Queen Angelfish, 50, 51
Queen Triggerfish, 72, 73

Red Hind, 30, 31
Redband Parrotfish, 70, 71

Redlip Blenny, 80, 81
Redspotted Hawkfish, 38, 39
Reef Butterflyfish, 55
Rock Beauty, 50, 51
Rock Hind, 30, 31

Sand Diver, 22, 23
Sergeant Major, 56, 57
Sharpnose Puffer, 78
Shortnose Batfish, 82, 83
Shy Hamlet, 32, 33
Slender Filefish, 76, 77
Slippery Dick, 66, 67
Smallmouth Grunt, 40, 41
Smooth Trunkfish, 76, 77
Soapfish, 34, 35
Spanish Hogfish, 62
Spiny Puffer, 78, 79
Spotfin Butterflyfish, 55
Spotted Drum, 46, 47
Spotted Goatfish, 44, 45
Spotted Moray, 20, 21

Spotted Scorpionfish, 80, 81
Spotted Trunkfish, 77
Squirrelfish, 24, 25
Stoplight Parrotfish, 68, 69
Striped Parrotfish, 70, 71

Threespot Damselfish, 60, 61
Tobacco Fish, 31
Tomtate, 42, 43
Trumpetfish, 22, 23

Web Burrfish, 78, 79
Wrasses, 62

Yellow Damselfish, 60, 61
Yellow Goatfish, 44, 45
Yellowbellied Hamlet, 32, 33
Yellow Edge Chromis, 56, 57
Yellowhead Jawfish, 44, 45
Yellowhead Wrasse, 64, 65
Yellowtail Damselfish, 59